EASY ANSWERS

TO FIRST SCIENCE QUESTIONS ABOUT

ANIMALS

WRITTEN BY Q. L. PEARCE

ILLUSTRATED BY GIL HUNG

EXPERT CONSULTANT: Anthony Valenzuela, Curator of Mammals,
Los Angeles Zoo, Los Angeles, California

TO RUBY PEARCE

SMITHMARK

An RGA Book

This edition published in 1991 by SMITHMARK Publishers Inc.,
112 Madison Avenue, New York, NY 10016.
Manufactured in the United States of America.

ISBN 0-8317-2584-2

Q: WHAT IS AN ANIMAL?

Answer: An animal is a living thing. Animals are different from other living things, such as plants, in several ways. An animal cannot make its own food. It must eat or feed usually upon plants or other animals. It then digests, or breaks down, the food within its own body. Unlike plants, an animal can move about freely during all or some part of its life.

Q: WHICH IS THE SMALLEST ANIMAL?

Answer: Earth's smallest animals belong to a group called the Protozoa (prot-uh-ZO-uh). These creatures may be so tiny that thousands and thousands of them could fit on this page! Many animals that are larger than protozoans are still very tiny. The smallest fish, the pygmy dwarf goby, is only about a third of an inch long. The hog-nosed bat, the world's tiniest mammal, rarely reaches more than 1½ inches from end to end.

The pygmy dwarf goby, shown five times larger than actual size

Q: WHAT IS AN INSECT?

Answer: An insect is an animal whose body is divided into three parts—the head, thorax (THOR-aks), and abdomen (AB-duh-mun). It has six legs and two antennae on its head, and many varieties of insects have one or two pairs of wings. Beetles, butterflies, moths, flies, ants, and bees are all types of insects.

Q: WHY ARE THERE NO GIANT INSECTS?

Answer: You may see giant ants as big as elephants in movies, but insects could never really grow that big. One important reason is because of the type of openings and air passages in an insect's body. These passages work well in a tiny animal, but they wouldn't work at all in larger creatures. Still, some insects are very large compared to others. One of the world's largest insects, the Hercules beetle of South America, can grow up to eight inches long.

The Hercules beetle is gigantic compared to the common ant

Q: Do insects have blood?

Answer: Yes, but an insect's blood is unlike that of a human. In humans, blood carries nutrients and oxygen, and it travels throughout the body in special "tubes" called blood vessels. An insect's blood carries nutrients but not oxygen. Instead of traveling only in vessels, the blood fills the insect's body. Because of this, the blood also provides "padding" between the animal's outer covering and its inner organs, such as the heart and stomach.

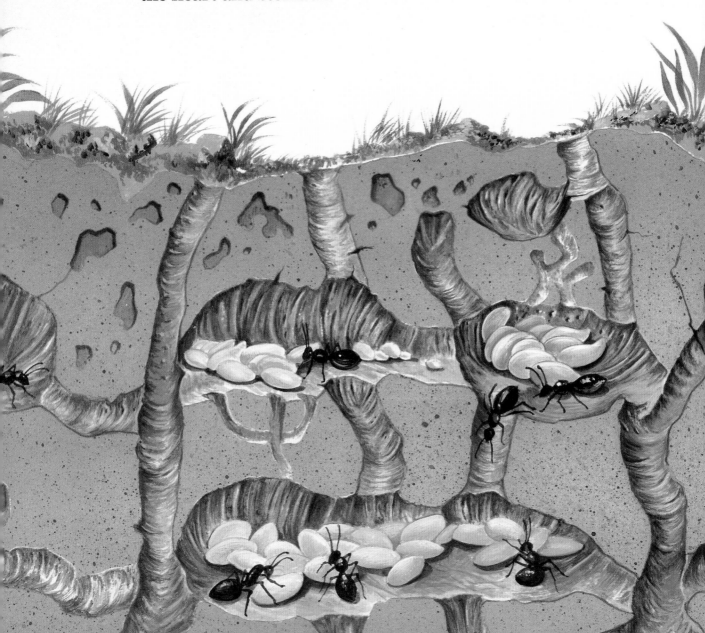

Q: DO INSECTS HAVE BONES?

Answer: No. Insects have an outer covering called an exoskeleton. The exoskeleton is made of a material much like that in your fingernails. It is coated with a thin, waxy, waterproof layer that helps to prevent water loss. The exoskeleton of some insects, such as beetles, is hard and stiff. Other insects, such as flies, have a soft, flexible exoskeleton.

Q: DO HONEY BEES LAY EGGS?

Answer: Only a queen honey bee lays eggs, and that is her only job. In each honey bee nest, or hive, there may be as many as 60,000 bees. Most are female workers. The workers clean and guard the hive, collect and store food, and care for the young. At certain times of the year, male bees are born. The males, called drones, are mates for the queen bee. There is usually only one queen in each hive, but she can lay up to 2,000 eggs a day.

Q: WHY DO HONEY BEES MAKE WAX?

Answer: Honey bees make wax in order to build storage units, called combs, in their hives. A comb is made up of many six-sided compartments, or cells, that are joined together. A worker bee produces the wax in special glands on her body. The bee scrapes the wax into a small ball and then chews it. Chewing makes the wax moldable so that the bee can form it into cells. The queen bee lays her eggs in these cells. The cells are also used for storing honey.

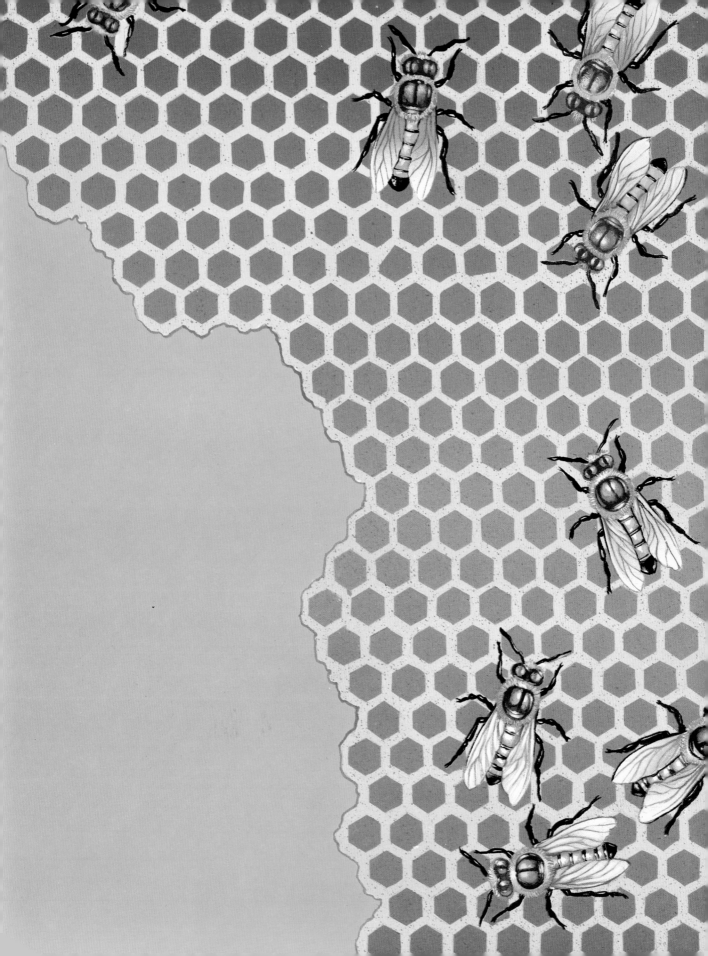

Q: *WHAT IS AN AMPHIBIAN?*

Answer: Generally, an amphibian (am-FIB-ee-un) is an animal, such as a frog or toad, that begins its life in water breathing through gills. Then, as an adult, it lives on land and breathes air through lungs. (A few kinds of amphibians continue to live in water even as adults.) Amphibians usually lay their shell-less eggs in or near water. The young that hatch from the eggs are called tadpoles.

Tadpole

Q: WHAT'S THE DIFFERENCE BETWEEN A FROG AND A TOAD?

Answer: Even though they are closely related, there are several differences between a frog and a toad. A frog has smooth, damp skin. A toad's skin is dry and bumpy. The legs of most types of frogs are long and slender, while toads often have fairly short, plump legs. The best place to look for a frog is in or near water. Toads usually live in damp places, but not necessarily close to a pond or stream.

Q: WHAT IS A REPTILE?

Answer: A reptile is an animal that has a backbone, breathes air, usually lays eggs, and is often covered by a layer of scales or plates. A reptile is cold-blooded. That means that it does not control its own body temperature. Instead, the temperature of a reptile's body changes with the temperature of its environment. Snakes, lizards, crocodiles, and turtles are all reptiles

Q: WHY DOES A LIZARD SHED ITS SKIN?

Answer: A lizard sheds its skin because its outer covering does not grow as the animal grows. Instead, the scaly covering becomes too small, just as your clothes become too small and no longer fit as *you* grow. (All reptiles, in fact, shed at least a portion of their outer coverings.) When its old skin becomes too tight, a lizard simply sheds it. Some, such as the alligator lizard, shed their skins in one piece. Others shed their coverings in ragged sheets. Some lizards even shed their skins one scale at a time! How often a lizard sheds depends on what kind of lizard it is.

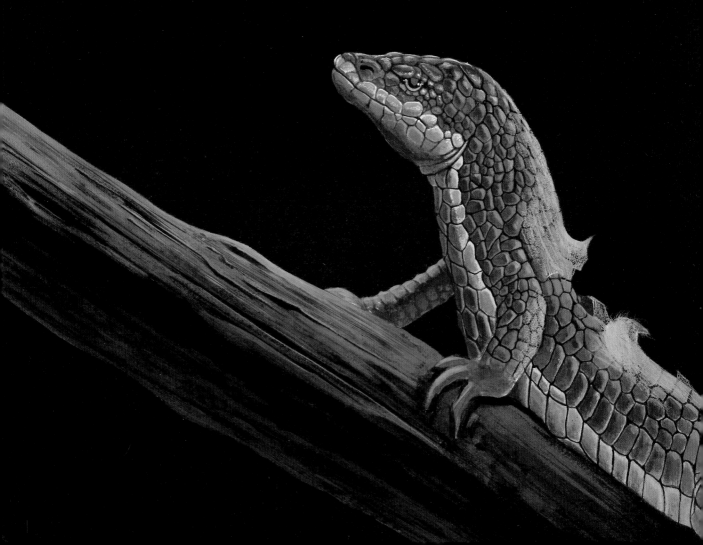

Q: DO SNAKES CHEW THEIR FOOD?

Answer: Snakes do not chew their food. Their teeth are designed for holding prey, not for chewing. Some snakes eat worms, insects, and eggs. Others eat birds, mammals, fish, and even other snakes. But no matter what sort of meal a snake has, it always swallows it whole. With its flexible jaws, a snake can open its mouth wide enough to gobble down a meal twice the size of its own head!

Q: WHY DO SNAKES STICK OUT THEIR TONGUES?

Answer: A snake uses its tongue to sense the world around it. As a snake moves, it sticks out its tongue to sample the air and ground. Then it draws the forked tongue back into its mouth and touches the tips to a special sense organ called Jacobson's organ. This organ enables the snake to taste and smell what is on its tongue. Using this special organ, a snake can avoid an enemy or track prey.

Q: *WHAT IS A BIRD?*

Answer: A bird is an egg-laying animal with a back-bone. It also is warm-blooded, which means its body temperature always remains nearly the same, no matter what the temperature of its surroundings. But the special feature that sets birds apart from all other animals is their covering of feathers. Many, but not all, birds can fly. The world's largest bird, the ostrich, cannot fly at all, but with a running speed of up to forty-five miles per hour, it can usually outrun its enemies.

Ostrich   Adult man

Q: WHY DON'T BIRDS FALL OUT OF TREES WHEN THEY SLEEP?

Answer: A bird's own weight helps to keep it in place while it sleeps. When a bird grips a branch with its toes, its weight pushes slightly forward. This causes tendons in the bird's feet to pull the toes together and lock the feet into position. The more relaxed the bird is, the farther forward it settles and the more secure its grip becomes. To let go of the branch, the bird simply straightens up.

Q: WHY DO BIRDS SING?

Answer: Not all birds sing, but those that do are often trying to attract a mate. Sometimes birds sing to announce their claim to a particular territory. Generally, it is the male bird that sings. He trills his special melody from a high perch or even in flight. Some of the bird songs most loved by humans are those of the meadowlark and nightingale.

Q: HOW DO PENGUINS STAY WARM?

Answer: A thick layer of fat under their skin and a covering of waterproof feathers help penguins to keep warm. Like other birds, a penguin is warm-blooded. The penguin's layer of fat, called blubber, and its tiny, tightly packed feathers enable it to retain heat. In fact, the penguin can survive in colder weather better than any other bird on Earth. When winter winds blow, some penguins stay warmer by huddling together.

Q: *WHAT IS A MAMMAL?*

Answer: A mammal is a warm-blooded, air-breathing animal that has a backbone and, usually, a covering of hair or fur. (Some mammals have very little hair. Whales, for instance, have only a few hairs on their lips, or none at all.) Female mammals produce milk to feed their young and most give birth to live, well-developed babies. Dogs, bats, elephants, mice, and humans are all mammals.

Q: WHY DO SOME ANIMALS SLEEP THROUGH THE WINTER?

Answer: Some animals sleep through the winter because the weather is very harsh, or because food is in short supply. When it is asleep, an animal uses less energy, needs far less food, and can survive on fat stored up in its body. Some animals, such as the ground squirrel, go into a state called hibernation. During hibernation, the animal's heart beats very slowly and its body temperature falls very low.

Q: WHY DO BATS SQUEAK?

Answer: Bats squeak for several different reasons. First, they squeak to communicate with each other. For example, the noisy animals call or bicker at each other in their roost until each finds a spot and settles down. Insect-eating bats also use sound as a kind of radar. When a flying bat squeaks, the sound bounces off objects in its path. The bat can tell from the returning sound where an object is and whether it is an insect.

Q: WHY DO BATS HANG UPSIDE DOWN?

Answer: By hanging high above the ground when resting, a bat stays safely out of reach of most of its predators. Because of the design of its legs (a bat's knees bend backward instead of forward), this animal is more comfortable when hanging upside down. Most bats have curved claws that serve as hooks from which to hang. A few kinds of bats have suckerlike discs on their toes that enable them to cling to smooth surfaces

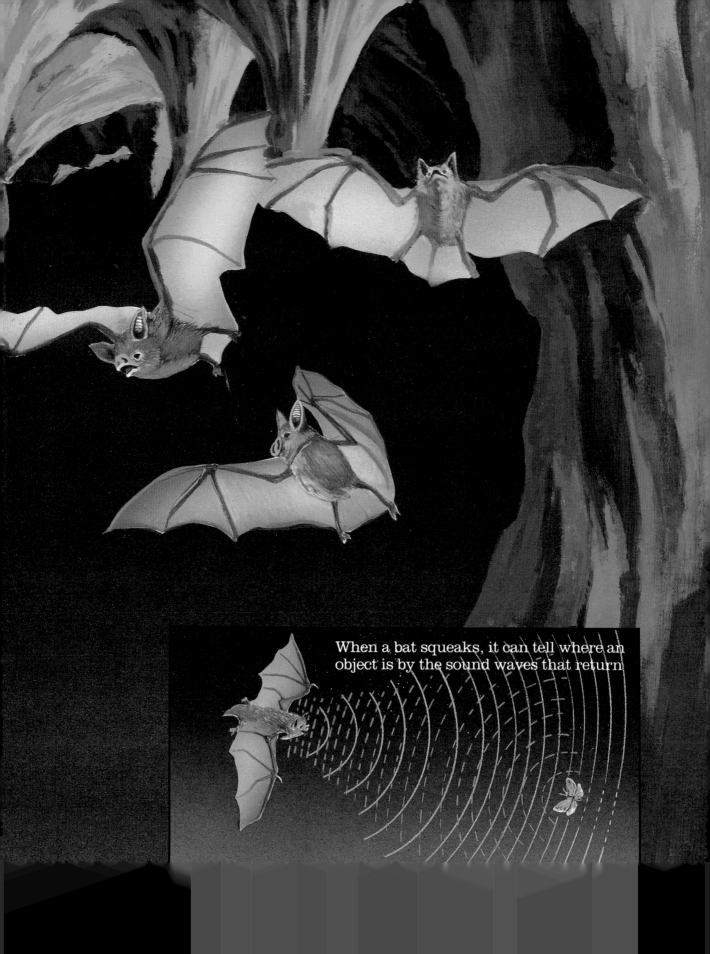

When a bat squeaks, it can tell where an object is by the sound waves that return

Q: WHY DOES A KANGAROO HAVE A POUCH?

Answer: Only the *female* kangaroo has a pouch, which serves as a safe place for her baby until it is old enough to take care of itself. At birth, a baby kangaroo (called a joey) is not fully developed. The newborn joey, less than an inch long, climbs through its mother's fur to her warm pouch, where it finds food and protection. Kangaroos are not the only animals with pouches. Female opossums and koala bears have them, too. Mammals with pouches are called marsupials (mar-SOO-pee-ulz).

Answer: Only two mammals, the duck-billed platypus (PLAT-ih-pus) and the echidna (ih-KID-nuh), lay eggs. Known as monotremes, both animals are found mainly in Australia. The female duck-billed platypus digs a tunnel in a riverbank, then lays her eggs in a grass-lined chamber in the tunnel. After hatching, the babies develop further in their mother's pouch. A baby echidna also spends about six weeks in its mother's pouch.

Q: DOES AN ELEPHANT DRINK THROUGH ITS TRUNK?

Answer: An elephant uses its trunk to get a drink, but it doesn't use it as a straw. The animal sucks water into its trunk, then squirts the water into its mouth to be swallowed. Sometimes the elephant uses its trunk to spray water over its back for a cooling shower. The trunk is an elephant's nose and upper lip combined. An elephant can use its trunk (which is equipped with *thousands* of different muscles) to pick up a heavy tree branch or to gently caress an elephant calf.

Q: WHY DO ZEBRAS HAVE STRIPES?

Answer: A zebra's distinctive black and white stripes are a kind of camouflage. The stripes may make this animal seem more obvious to humans, but they confuse predators such as lions. One theory is that the pattern breaks up the zebra's outline, causing the creature to blend in with its background. Because no two zebras are patterned exactly alike, the stripes may also help the animals to identify each other.

Q: DO ALL CATS PURR?

Answer: Not all members of the cat family purr.
Smaller cats, such as the lynx and particularly the
house cat, are able to purr. House cats purr when they
are happy or content. The sound is produced by blood
moving quickly through a special vein in the cat's
chest. The "great cats," such as jaguars, cheetahs,
lions, leopards, and tigers, do not purr. Instead, these
powerful members of the cat family snarl, growl,
and roar.

Q: DO ALL MONKEYS SWING FROM THEIR TAILS?

Answer: No. Tails that are used to wrap around or grip branches, enabling a monkey to swing from them, are called prehensile. The word prehensile means "able to grasp." Adult monkeys of Africa and Asia generally do not have prehensile tails. Many South American monkeys, including the woolly monkey and the spider monkey, do have this type of long, flexible tail. They use it almost like a fifth "hand" as they scamper high in the treetops.

Q: WHY CAN'T ANIMALS TALK TO US?

Answer: Animals cannot talk to us in clear, human language because they do not have vocal cords like those of humans, and most do not have the sort of muscles needed to control speech. However, in some ways animals do "talk" to us. When a dog wags its tail, you know it is happy. When it growls and shows its teeth, you know it may be angry or frightened. Animals use not only sound, but also sight and scent to communicate with us and with each other.

Q: WHAT IS EXTINCTION?

Answer: When a type of animal has died out completely, we say that it has become extinct. Extinction is a natural part of life on Earth. A group of animals may die out when its environment changes. Perhaps the weather becomes too cold or too dry, or the food source disappears. When we humans change the environment to suit our needs, we must be careful to protect our fellow creatures and their habitats so that no animal becomes extinct unnecessarily.

Here are several other questions to consider about animals.

WHERE DO INSECTS LIVE?
DO ALL INSECTS HAVE WINGS?
HOW MANY DIFFERENT KINDS OF INSECTS ARE THERE?
HOW LONG DO INSECTS LIVE?
WHAT IS THE DIFFERENCE BETWEEN A SPIDER AND AN INSECT?
ARE SOME AMPHIBIANS POISONOUS?
WHAT'S THE DIFFERENCE BETWEEN AN ALLIGATOR AND A CROCODILE?
CAN A TURTLE GET OUT OF ITS SHELL?
DO BABY BIRDS KNOW HOW TO FLY?
HOW FAST CAN THE FASTEST BIRD FLY?
WHAT ARE BIRDS' NESTS MADE OF?
HOW IS AN APE DIFFERENT FROM A MONKEY?

These books will help you discover the answers:

Attmore, Stephen: *Animal Encyclopedia*, Newmarket, England, Brimax Books, 1987.

National Wildlife Federation: *The Unhuggables*, Washington, D.C., 1988.

Staple, Michele, and Gamlin, Linda: *The Random House Book of 1001 Questions and Answers About Animals*, New York City, Random House, 1990.

Sussman, Susan, and James, Robert: *Lies People Believe About Animals*, Niles, Illinois, Albert Whitman & Company, 1987.